CHRISTMAS AT HOME
Traditional Family Favorites

BARBOUR
PUBLISHING

CONTENTS

YULETIDE BEVERAGES

Love came down at Christmas
Love all lovely, love divine;
Love was born at Christmas,
Stars and angels gave the sign.

CHRISTINA ROSSETTI

PARSONAGE PUNCH

8 regular tea bags
2 cups boiling water
1½ cups sugar
2 slices fresh lemon
1½ teaspoons almond flavoring
1½ teaspoons vanilla
1 (2 liter) bottle lemon-lime soda

Steep tea bags in water for 20 minutes. Remove tea bags. Add sugar and lemon slices.
Refrigerate overnight. Add flavorings, soda, and ice. Serve. Yield: 25 punch cups

HOLIDAY WASSAIL

1 quart hot tea
1 cup sugar
1 (32 ounce) bottle cranberry juice
1 (32 ounce) bottle apple juice
2 cups orange juice
¾ cup lemon juice
2 cinnamon sticks
12 whole cloves, divided
1 orange, sliced

In a large kettle, combine tea and sugar. Add juices. Insert cinnamon sticks and 12 cloves into spice bag. Add spice bag to juice mixture. Bring to a boil, reduce heat, cover, and simmer 20 to 30 minutes. Remove spice bag and discard. Serve warm. Garnish punch bowl with clove studded orange slices or sliced apples.

MOCHA PUNCH

1½ quarts water
½ cup instant chocolate drink mix
½ cup sugar
¼ cup instant coffee granules
½ gallon vanilla ice cream
½ gallon chocolate ice cream

In large saucepan, bring water to a boil. Remove from heat. Add drink mix, sugar, and coffee; stir until dissolved. Cover and refrigerate for 4 hours or overnight. About 30 minutes before serving, pour into punch bowl. Add ice cream by scoopfuls and stir until partially melted. Yield: 20 to 25 servings

CREAMY DREAMY HOT CHOCOLATE

1 (14 ounce) can sweetened condensed milk
½ cup unsweetened cocoa powder
2 teaspoons vanilla
⅛ teaspoon salt
6½ cups hot water

Combine first 4 ingredients in large saucepan; mix well. Over medium heat, slowly stir in water. Cook until heated through, stirring frequently.

OLD-TIMER'S EGGNOG

6 eggs, slightly beaten
4 cups whole milk
¼ cup sugar
¼ teaspoon salt
2 cups whipping cream or 1 pint vanilla ice cream
Dash nutmeg
Peppermint sticks

In a large saucepan, mix eggs, milk, sugar, and salt. Cook and stir over medium heat until mixture coats a metal spoon. Remove from heat. Fold in whipping cream or ice cream. Pour into punch bowl or pitcher. Cover and refrigerate overnight. Sprinkle each serving with nutmeg. Serve with a peppermint stick.

CRANBERRY PUNCH

1 (64 ounce) bottle cranberry juice cocktail
1 (48 ounce) bottle pineapple juice
¼ cup lemon juice
1 cup sugar
1 cup grapefruit juice
4 liters of ginger ale

Mix ingredients together well and add ice. Yield: 10 to 12 servings

DELIGHTFUL DIPS & APPETIZERS

*It is Christmas in the heart that
puts Christmas in the air.*

W. T. ELLIS

HONEY-GLAZED CHICKEN WINGS

3 pounds chicken wings
⅛ cup soy sauce
2 tablespoons vegetable oil
2 tablespoons chili sauce (or ketchup or barbecue sauce)
¼ cup honey
1 teaspoon salt
½ teaspoon ginger
¼ teaspoon garlic powder (or 1 clove garlic, minced)
¼ teaspoon cayenne pepper

Separate wings at joints. Mix remaining ingredients. Pour over chicken. Cover and refrigerate, turning chicken occasionally, at least 1 hour or overnight. Heat oven to 375 degrees. Drain chicken, reserving marinade. Place chicken on rack in foil-lined broiler pan. Bake for 30 minutes. Brush chicken with reserved marinade. Turn chicken and bake for another 30 minutes or until tender.

HOT ARTICHOKE AND SPINACH DIP

$\frac{1}{2}$ cup sour cream
$\frac{1}{2}$ cup mayonnaise
$\frac{1}{2}$ cup Parmesan cheese, grated
$\frac{1}{2}$ cup mozzarella cheese, shredded
1 to 2 teaspoons garlic, minced
1 package frozen spinach, thawed and well drained
1 (14 ounce) can artichoke hearts, drained

Combine all ingredients. Place in shallow casserole dish. Bake at 325 degrees for 15 to 20 minutes or until bubbly.

MEXICAN FIESTA DIP

1 can bean dip
2 large ripe avocados
1 teaspoon lemon juice
Dash garlic salt
1 small onion, chopped
½ cup salsa

1 large tomato, chopped
1 cup sour cream
1 package dry taco seasoning
½ cup mayonnaise
1 to 2 cups cheddar cheese

Spread bean dip in bottom of 9x9-inch dish. Scoop out avocados, discarding skins. Blend avocado in food processor or mash with a fork. Add lemon juice, garlic salt, onions, salsa, and half of tomatoes. Spread over bean dip. Mix sour cream, mayonnaise, and taco seasoning. Spread over avocado mixture. Place cheese and remaining tomatoes on top. Serve with corn chips or tortilla chips.

CRANBERRY DELIGHT HOLIDAY SPREAD

1 (8 ounce) package cream cheese, softened
2 tablespoons orange juice concentrate
1 tablespoon sugar
⅛ teaspoon cinnamon
Zest of 1 orange
¼ cup dried cranberries
¼ cup pecans, chopped

Beat cream cheese, orange juice, sugar, and cinnamon in medium mixing bowl. Stir in zest, cranberries, and pecans. Chill. Delicious served with chocolate-covered pretzels, crackers, or on a bagel.

RYE BREAD DIP

1 box frozen chopped spinach, well drained
1 envelope vegetable soup mix
1 cup sour cream
1 cup mayonnaise
1 onion, chopped fine
1 can water chestnuts, chopped and drained
1 loaf rye bread (round)

Mix together all ingredients, except rye bread, and refrigerate until cold. Hollow out center of rye loaf. Spoon chilled dip into center of bread. Cut up removed center piece of bread into bite-size pieces and use for dipping. Also tastes great on crackers.

FRUIT DIP

1 (7 ounce) jar marshmallow crème
2 (8 ounce) packages cream cheese, softened
1 teaspoon lemon juice

Mix together and serve with fresh fruit.

DILL VEGETABLE DIP

1 cup sour cream
1 cup mayonnaise
1 tablespoon onion, chopped
1 tablespoon dill weed
1 tablespoon parsley flakes
1 teaspoon seasoned salt

Mix and chill several hours or overnight. Serve with your favorite fresh veggies.

HOT CHIPPED BEEF DIP

1 (2½ ounce) package dried beef
1 (8 ounce) package cream cheese, softened
2 tablespoons milk
½ cup sour cream
2 teaspoons onion, minced
½ teaspoon garlic salt
¼ teaspoon pepper

Topping:
½ cup pecans, chopped
1 tablespoon butter
½ teaspoon salt

Cut up beef and mix with rest of dip ingredients. Place in 1-quart baking dish. Sauté topping ingredients in skillet over low heat. Sprinkle on top of dip and bake at 350 degrees for 20 minutes. Serve with your favorite crackers.

DELICIOUS STUFFED MUSHROOMS

1 pound large fresh mushrooms
⅓ cup butter, softened
4½ teaspoons flour
1 tablespoon onion, finely chopped
1 tablespoon fresh parsley, minced
1 tablespoon Dijon mustard
½ teaspoon salt
⅛ teaspoon cayenne pepper
Dash ground mustard
1 cup heavy whipping cream

Remove stems from mushrooms; set caps aside. Finely chop stems. Combine butter, flour, onion, parsley, mustard, salt, cayenne pepper, mustard, and chopped stems. Fill mushroom caps with mixture. Place in shallow, greased 2-quart baking dish. Pour cream over mushrooms. Bake, uncovered, at 375 degrees for 30 to 35 minutes or until mushrooms are tender, basting twice. Yield: about 2 dozen

PEPPERONI PIZZA SPREAD

2 cups mozzarella cheese, shredded
2 cups cheddar cheese, shredded
1 cup mayonnaise
1 cup pepperoni, chopped
1 (4 ounce) can mushrooms, drained and chopped
½ cup onion, chopped
½ cup green pepper, chopped
1 (6 ounce) can ripe olives, drained and chopped

Combine all ingredients. Spread in 7x11-inch baking dish. Bake uncovered at 350 degrees for 25 to 30 minutes or until edges are bubbly and lightly browned. Serve with crackers, bread sticks, or French bread.

PEPPER POPPERS

1 (8 ounce) package cream cheese,
    softened
1 cup cheddar cheese, shredded
1 cup Monterey Jack cheese, shredded
6 bacon strips, cooked and crumbled
¼ teaspoon salt
¼ teaspoon chili powder

¼ teaspoon garlic powder
1 pound fresh jalapenos, halved
    lengthwise and seeded*
½ cup dry bread crumbs
Sour cream, onion dip, or ranch
    salad dressing

Combine cheeses, bacon, and seasonings; mix well. Spoon about 2 tablespoons into each pepper half. Roll in bread crumbs. Place in greased 10x15-inch baking pan. Bake, uncovered, at 300 degrees for 20 minutes for spicy flavor, 30 minutes for medium, and 40 minutes for mild. Serve with sour cream, dip, or dressing.

When working with hot peppers, wear plastic gloves and avoid touching face.

OLIVE CORN SPREAD

1 (8 ounce) package cream cheese, softened
1 (1 ounce) envelope ranch dressing mix
1 (11 ounce) can whole kernel corn, drained
1¼ cups black olives, chopped
1 medium red pepper, chopped

Combine cream cheese and ranch dressing mix. Beat until smooth. Add remaining ingredients and mix well. Refrigerate 1 to 1½ hours before serving. Serve with tortilla chips.

GRANDMA'S CARAMEL CORN

1 cup butter or margarine
2 cups brown sugar
½ cup light corn syrup
1 teaspoon salt
1 teaspoon vanilla
½ teaspoon baking soda
24 cups popcorn, popped

In medium saucepan, melt butter; stir in brown sugar, corn syrup, and salt. Bring to a boil and boil 5 minutes. Do not stir. Remove from heat. Stir in vanilla and soda. Measure popcorn into lightly greased roasting pan. Pour caramel sauce over popcorn, stirring until popcorn is coated. Bake at 250 degrees for 1 hour, stirring every 15 minutes.

CHRISTMAS BRUNCH

O little town of Bethlehem,
How still we see thee lie;
Above thy deep and dreamless sleep
The silent stars go by.

PHILLIPS BROOKS

CHEESE DANISH

2 tubes crescent rolls
2 (8 ounce) packages
   cream cheese, softened
1 teaspoon vanilla
1 cup sugar
3 tablespoons butter,
   melted

Topping:
1 teaspoon cinnamon
½ cup sugar

Glaze:
1½ cups powdered sugar
2 to 3 tablespoons milk

Layer 1 package of rolls on bottom of a 9x13-inch ungreased pan. Pat seams closed. Beat cream cheese, vanilla, and sugar until smooth. Spread cream cheese mixture over crescent rolls. Place second package of crescent rolls on top. Drizzle with butter. Mix cinnamon and sugar; sprinkle over top. Bake at 350 degrees for 30 to 35 minutes. Combine glaze ingredients; drizzle over top of pastry. Cool.

BAKED OATMEAL

½ cup butter, melted
¾ cup brown sugar
2 eggs, slightly beaten
1 teaspoon salt
3 cups quick oatmeal
1½ teaspoons cinnamon
2 teaspoons baking powder
1 cup milk
1 teaspoon vanilla

Mix everything together and pour into greased 8x8-inch baking dish. Bake at 350 degrees for 25 to 30 minutes. Serve warm with vanilla yogurt and fruit. Variations: add raisins, dried cranberries, and nuts. Also try adding coconut and pecans to batter and top with vanilla yogurt after oatmeal batter is baked.

PECAN FRENCH TOAST BAKE

1 loaf French bread, cut into
    1-inch slices
8 eggs
2 cups half & half
2 cups milk
½ teaspoon nutmeg
2 teaspoons vanilla
½ teaspoon cinnamon

Topping:
¾ cup butter, softened
3 tablespoons corn syrup
1⅓ cups brown sugar
1 cup pecans, chopped

Place bread slices in greased 9x13-inch baking dish. Blend eggs, milk, half & half, vanilla, nutmeg, and cinnamon. Pour mixture over bread slices. Cover and refrigerate overnight. Mix topping ingredients and spread over bread slices. Bake at 350 degrees for 50 minutes or until puffed and golden brown. Serve with or without syrup.

HANNAH'S HOUSE BREAKFAST CASSEROLE

1 pound fresh sausage
2 cups cheddar cheese, shredded
6 eggs, lightly beaten
1 cup water
½ cup milk
½ cup country gravy mix
6 slices bread, cut into 1-inch cubes
2 tablespoons butter, melted

Brown sausage; drain. Layer sausage in bottom of greased 8x11-inch baking dish. Top with cheese. Whisk together eggs, water, milk, and gravy mix; pour over cheese. Arrange bread cubes evenly on top; drizzle butter over bread. Bake 30 to 40 minutes or until a knife inserted in center comes out clean. Sprinkle with parsley or chives. Cut in squares. Serve immediately. Yield: 6 servings

HASH BROWN BAKE

4 cups frozen shredded potatoes
½ cup butter, melted
½ cup Parmesan cheese
1 small onion, diced
2 cups ham, diced
2 cups cheddar cheese, shredded
8 eggs

1 cup milk
1 clove garlic, minced
Salt and pepper to taste

Thaw potatoes and blot with paper towel to remove excess moisture. Press potatoes into bottom of greased 9x13-inch baking dish. Drizzle with butter and sprinkle with Parmesan cheese. Bake at 425 degrees for 25 minutes. Cool on wire rack 10 minutes. Mix onion, ham, and cheddar cheese and spread mixture over potatoes. Combine eggs, milk, garlic, salt, and pepper; pour over ham mixture. Bake at 350 degrees for 30 minutes or until set. Let stand 10 minutes before serving.

HAM AND CHEESE QUICHE

1 teaspoon butter, melted
1⅓ cups Swiss cheese, finely grated
1 cup ham, diced
¾ cup sour cream
¼ cup mayonnaise
½ teaspoon salt
1 teaspoon flour
1 cup light cream or half & half
3 eggs, slightly beaten
½ teaspoon hot pepper sauce

Mix ingredients and pour into a 10-inch unbaked pie shell. Bake at 350 degrees on lower oven rack for 55 minutes or until set. Let stand 10 minutes before serving. Can also be prepared with mushrooms, bacon, spinach, or tomatoes. If using fresh mushrooms, tomatoes, or spinach, sauté in the butter first and drain off excess moisture.

CRANBERRY CREAM COFFEE CAKE

2 cups flour
1 cup sugar
1½ teaspoons baking powder
½ teaspoon baking soda
1 egg
¾ cup orange juice
¼ cup butter, softened
1 teaspoon vanilla
2 cups fresh cranberries, coarsely
  chopped
1 tablespoon orange zest

Cream Cheese Layer:
1 (8 ounce) package cream cheese,
  softened
⅓ cup sugar
1 egg
1 teaspoon vanilla

Topping:
¾ cup flour
½ cup sugar
½ cup cold butter

Combine first 4 ingredients. Mix together egg, orange juice, butter, and vanilla; stir into dry ingredients until well blended. Fold in cranberries and orange zest. Pour into greased 9-inch springform pan. In small bowl, beat cream cheese and sugar until smooth. Add egg and vanilla; mix well. Spoon over batter. For topping; combine flour and sugar. Cut in butter until mixture resembles coarse crumbs. Sprinkle over top. Place pan on baking sheet. Bake at 350 degrees for 1 hour or until golden brown. Cool on wire rack for 15 minutes before releasing sides of pan.

PUMPKIN MAPLE COFFEE CAKE

1½ cups flour
¾ cup brown sugar
2 teaspoons baking powder
½ teaspoon salt
¼ teaspoon baking soda
⅔ cup buttermilk
½ cup canned pumpkin
⅓ cup oil

½ teaspoon maple flavoring
2 eggs, beaten

Topping:
½ cup sugar
1 teaspoon cinnamon
1 teaspoon maple flavoring

Combine flour, sugar, baking powder, salt, and baking soda. Whisk until well blended. Combine buttermilk, pumpkin, oil, maple flavoring, and eggs. Mix well. Add to dry ingredients and blend just until dry ingredients are moistened. In small bowl, combine topping ingredients; mix well with fork. Spread half of batter in greased 9x9-inch baking pan. Sprinkle with half of topping. Spoon remaining batter over top; spread evenly. Sprinkle with remaining topping. Bake at 350 degrees for 25 to 35 minutes or until toothpick inserted in center comes out clean. Cool 15 minutes. Serve warm.

GINGER APPLE MUFFINS

2 cups flour
1/4 cup brown sugar
1 teaspoon ginger
1 teaspoon baking soda
1 teaspoon cinnamon
1/4 teaspoon salt
1 cup applesauce
1/2 cup oil
1/2 cup molasses
1 egg

Topping:
2 tablespoons flour
2 tablespoons brown sugar
1/2 teaspoon cinnamon
1 tablespoon butter, softened
1 tablespoon walnuts, chopped

Line a 12-muffin pan with paper baking cups. Combine flour, brown sugar, ginger, baking soda, cinnamon, and salt; blend well with whisk. In medium bowl, combine applesauce, oil, molasses, and egg; blend well. Add to dry ingredients; stir just until dry ingredients are moistened. Divide batter between cups. Combine topping ingredients. Sprinkle over batter. Bake at 400 degrees for 18 to 20 minutes.

LEMON RASPBERRY STREUSEL MUFFINS

2 cups flour
$\frac{1}{2}$ cup sugar
2 teaspoons baking soda
$\frac{1}{2}$ teaspoon salt
1 (8 ounce) carton lemon yogurt
$\frac{1}{2}$ cup oil
Zest of 1 lemon
2 eggs

1 cup fresh or frozen raspberries,
   unthawed

Topping:
$\frac{1}{3}$ cup sugar
$\frac{1}{4}$ cup flour
2 tablespoons butter, softened

Line a 12-muffin pan with paper baking cups. Combine flour, sugar, baking soda, and salt; blend well with whisk. In small bowl, whisk yogurt, oil, lemon zest, and eggs; mix well. Add to dry ingredients; stir just until dry ingredients are moistened. Gently fold in raspberries. Fill muffin cups ¾ full. Combine topping ingredients with fork until crumbly. Spoon over batter. Bake at 400 degrees for 18 to 20 minutes.

RHUBARB BRUNCH CAKE

1 (18 ounce) box yellow cake mix
1 cup water
⅓ cup oil
3 eggs
4 cups fresh or frozen rhubarb, unthawed
1 cup sugar
2 cups whipping cream

Combine cake mix, water, oil, and eggs at low speed until moistened. Beat 2 minutes at highest speed. Pour into greased 9x13-inch baking pan. Top with rhubarb. Sprinkle with sugar. Pour cream over batter. Bake at 350 degrees for 60 to 70 minutes or until toothpick inserted in center comes out clean. Serve warm with additional whipped cream.

ALMOND POPPY SEED LOAF

3 cups flour
2½ cups sugar
1½ teaspoons salt
1½ teaspoons baking powder
1½ tablespoons poppy seeds
3 eggs
1½ cups milk
1⅓ cups oil
1½ teaspoons vanilla
1½ teaspoons almond flavoring
6 tablespoons butter, melted

Glaze:
2 tablespoons butter, melted
½ teaspoon almond flavoring
½ teaspoon vanilla
½ cup orange juice
¾ cup sugar

Whisk together flour, sugar, salt, baking powder, and poppy seeds. In a separate bowl, whisk eggs, milk, oil, vanilla, almond flavoring, and butter. Combine wet and dry ingredients and blend well. Divide batter into 2 greased 9x5-inch bread pans. Bake at 350 degrees for 40 to 50 minutes. Remove from oven and use toothpick to poke holes in top of bread. Mix glaze ingredients and pour slowly over hot bread, allowing it to run into holes. Let bread cool in pans. Remove from pans and slice.

Note: Best made a day before serving. Loaves are moister the second day.

FRUIT SLUSH

2 cups sugar
3 cups boiling water
12 ounces frozen orange juice concentrate
6 to 8 bananas, sliced
1 (20 ounce) can crushed pineapple, undrained
1 (8 ounce) can lemon-lime soda

Dissolve sugar in boiling water. Add orange juice concentrate, bananas, and pineapple, stirring until orange juice is dissolved. Stir in soda. Pour into large container or several small containers and freeze. Thaw in refrigerator approximately 1 hour or until slushy. Serve. Optional seasonal fruits may be added.

CRANBERRY ORANGE SCONES WITH ORANGE HONEY BUTTER

2 cups flour
1 tablespoon sugar
2 teaspoons baking powder
½ teaspoon salt
¼ cup butter

½ cup heavy cream
1 egg
1 cup dried cranberries
2 teaspoons orange zest
Additional sugar

Combine dry ingredients in large bowl. Work butter into dry ingredients with pastry blender or fork until butter is the size of small peas. Add remaining ingredients, except sugar, mixing just until dry ingredients are moistened. Turn dough onto a well-floured surface and gather into a ball. Pat into a circle ¾ inch thick; cut into 8 wedges. Place on cookie sheet. Sprinkle with sugar. Bake at 425 degrees 10 to 12 minutes or until golden brown. Serve scones warm with Orange Honey Butter (page 46).

ORANGE HONEY BUTTER

¼ cup butter, softened
½ tablespoon honey
½ teaspoon orange zest

In small bowl, cream butter until light and fluffy. Add honey and orange zest.

HEARTY SOUPS & SANDWICHES

For unto us a child is born, unto us a son is given: and the government shall be upon his shoulder: and his name shall be called Wonderful, Counselor, The mighty God, The everlasting Father, The Prince of Peace.

ISAIAH 9:6 KJV

WALDORF TURKEY SANDWICHES

1¼ cups cooked turkey breast, cubed
1 small apple, chopped
¼ cup celery, diced
3 tablespoons mayonnaise
2 tablespoons plain yogurt
2 tablespoons walnuts, chopped
1 tablespoon raisins
⅛ teaspoon nutmeg
⅛ teaspoon cinnamon
8 slices raisin bread, toasted
4 lettuce leaves

In a bowl, combine first 9 ingredients. Cover and refrigerate for 1 hour. Spoon turkey mixture onto bread slices; top with lettuce leaf and remaining bread. Yield: 4 servings

MONTE CRISTO SANDWICHES

8 slices sourdough bread
3 tablespoons Dijon mustard
½ pound thinly sliced deli ham
4 thin slices Swiss cheese
½ pound thinly sliced deli turkey or
 chicken breast

4 thin slices Provolone cheese
2 eggs, beaten
2 tablespoons milk
1 cup crushed crispy rice cereal
Powdered sugar
Strawberry or raspberry jam

Spread one side of each bread slice with Dijon mustard. Divide meats and cheeses to make 4 sandwiches. In shallow bowl, combine egg and milk; beat well. Place crushed cereal on shallow plate. Dip each sandwich briefly in egg mixture, then into cereal mixture to coat. Grill sandwiches on panini grill or fry with butter in skillet until crisp and brown. Sprinkle hot sandwiches with powdered sugar and serve with jam for dipping.

CURRIED CHICKEN CROISSANTS

2 cups chicken, cooked and cubed
1 medium apple, unpeeled and chopped
¾ cup dried cranberries
½ cup celery, finely diced
¼ cup pecans, chopped
½ cup grapes, halved
2 tablespoons green onion, finely chopped
¾ cup mayonnaise or salad dressing
2 teaspoons lime juice
½ teaspoon curry powder
Croissants

Combine the first 7 ingredients. Mix mayonnaise, lime juice, and curry powder in small bowl. Add to chicken mixture and stir to coat. Cover and refrigerate for several hours. Serve on toasted croissants. Lettuce leaves may be added.

CREAMED CHICKEN SANDWICHES

5 cups shredded chicken or turkey
2 (14½ ounce) cans chicken broth
1 sleeve wheat townhouse crackers, crushed
½ sleeve soda crackers, crushed
3 stalks celery, chopped
1 small onion, chopped
1 (10¾ ounce) cream of chicken soup
1 tablespoon mayonnaise
Salt and pepper to taste

Mix all ingredients in greased slow cooker and simmer on low 5 to 6 hours. Serve on buns. Yield:10 to 12 sandwiches

MAINE CORN CHOWDER

6 slices bacon
1 medium onion, diced
¼ cup butter
3 cups peeled potatoes, diced
1 cup celery, diced
2 cups water
1 teaspoon salt
½ teaspoon pepper
2 (17 ounce) cans cream-style corn
2 cups milk

Fry bacon in Dutch oven until crisp. Drain on paper towel. Set aside. Sauté onion in butter until soft. Add potatoes, celery, water, salt, and pepper. Bring to boil. Reduce heat. Cover and simmer about 15 minutes until potatoes and celery are tender. Add corn and milk. Heat thoroughly. When serving, garnish with crumbled bacon.

WHITE CHICKEN CHILI

1 pound boneless skinless chicken
    breasts, cut into $\frac{1}{2}$-inch cubes
1 medium onion, chopped
$1\frac{1}{2}$ teaspoons garlic powder
1 tablespoon vegetable oil
2 ($15\frac{1}{2}$ ounce) cans great northern
    beans, drained and rinsed
1 ($14\frac{1}{2}$ ounce) can chicken broth

2 (4 ounce) cans chopped green chilies
1 teaspoon salt
1 teaspoon cumin
1 teaspoon dried oregano
$\frac{1}{2}$ teaspoon pepper
$\frac{1}{4}$ teaspoon cayenne pepper
1 cup sour cream
$\frac{1}{2}$ cup heavy whipping cream

In large saucepan, sauté chicken, onion, and garlic powder in oil until chicken is no longer pink. Add beans, broth, chilies, and seasonings. Bring to boil. Reduce heat; simmer uncovered for 30 minutes. Remove from heat; stir in sour cream and heavy whipping cream. Heat through; do not boil.

SPLIT PEA SOUP

1 small onion, diced
1 tablespoon vegetable oil
4 cups water
1 (4½ ounce) can chicken broth
2 cups dry split peas, rinsed
1 cup fully cooked ham, cubed
3 bay leaves
1½ teaspoons salt
½ teaspoon dried rosemary, crushed
¼ teaspoon dried thyme
¼ teaspoon pepper

In large saucepan, sauté onion in oil until tender. Add remaining ingredients. Bring to boil; reduce heat. Cover and simmer for 1 hour or until peas are tender. Discard bay leaves. Yield: 6 servings

FRENCH ONION SOUP

4 medium onions, thinly sliced
4 tablespoons butter
$\frac{1}{2}$ teaspoon sugar
1$\frac{1}{2}$ cups chicken broth
1$\frac{1}{2}$ cups beef broth
1 to 2 ounces cooking sherry
1 bay leaf

$\frac{1}{8}$ teaspoon thyme
$\frac{1}{8}$ teaspoon Worcestershire sauce
pepper to taste
4 slices French bread, $\frac{1}{4}$- to $\frac{1}{2}$-inch
  slices, toasted
4 slices Swiss cheese
$\frac{1}{2}$ cup Parmesan cheese, grated

Melt butter and sauté onions until transparent. Add sugar and continue cooking until onions are caramelized and tender, about 10 minutes. Add broth, sherry, bay leaf, thyme, Worcestershire sauce, and pepper. Bring to boil; reduce heat and simmer, partially covered, for 15 to 20 minutes. Remove bay leaf. Place 4 ovenproof serving bowls on a baking sheet. Ladle soup into bowls. Place 1 bread slice on soup. Top with one cheese slice. Sprinkle each with Parmesan cheese. Broil 6 inches from heat until cheese is melted. Yield: 4 servings

SPICY CHEESEBURGER SOUP

1½ cups water
2 cups potatoes, peeled and cubed
2 small carrots, grated
1 small onion, chopped
1 small green pepper, chopped
1 jalapeno pepper, seeded and chopped*
1 garlic clove, minced
1 tablespoon beef bouillon granules
½ teaspoon salt
1 pound ground beef, cooked and drained
2½ cups milk, divided
3 tablespoons flour
8 ounces American cheese, cubed
¼ teaspoon cayenne pepper
½ pound sliced bacon, cooked and crumbled

In large saucepan, combine first 9 ingredients; bring to a boil. Reduce heat; cover and simmer for 15 to 20 minutes or until potatoes are tender. Stir in beef and 2 cups milk; heat through. Combine flour and remaining milk until smooth; gradually stir into soup. Bring to a boil; cook and stir for 2 minutes or until thickened and bubbly. Reduce heat; stir in cheeses until melted. Add cayenne if desired. Top with bacon just before serving. Yield: 6 to 8 servings

When working with hot peppers, wear plastic gloves and avoid touching face.

MOM'S PUMPKIN PATCH PEANUT BUTTER SOUP

3 tablespoons butter
½ cup onion, minced
4 cups canned pumpkin
3 cups chicken stock or broth
⅓ cup smooth peanut butter
¼ teaspoon cayenne pepper
1 teaspoon salt
½ teaspoon nutmeg
2 cups light cream or half & half

Melt butter in large saucepan, add onions; cook until soft. Add pumpkin, stock, peanut butter, cayenne pepper, salt, and nutmeg. Cook, stirring until peanut butter is melted and mixture is thoroughly heated. Stir in cream and warm through. Do not boil. Sprinkle with chives. Yield: 8 servings

SPINACH TORTELLINI SOUP

3 tablespoons olive oil
1 large onion, chopped
1 celery stalk, finely chopped
3 garlic cloves, minced
1 teaspoon dried basil
½ teaspoon salt
2 to 3 cups spinach or Swiss chard, stemmed and chopped

6 cups chicken broth
1 (9 ounce) package fresh cheese or meat tortellini
1 cup canned chickpeas, drained and rinsed
1 tablespoon tomato paste
Coarsely ground fresh pepper
Parmesan cheese, grated

Heat oil in large saucepan over medium heat. Add onion, celery, garlic, basil, and salt. Sauté for 5 minutes, stirring frequently. Add spinach and continue cooking until greens are wilted (4 to 5 minutes). Add broth and bring to boil. Add tortellini, chickpeas, tomato paste, and pepper. Return soup to boil. Reduce heat to medium-low and simmer, partially covered, 5 minutes. Garnish with Parmesan cheese. Serves 6.

STUFFED PEPPER SOUP

2 pounds ground beef
1 small onion, chopped
2 cloves garlic, chopped
2 green peppers, chopped
1 (29 ounce) can tomato sauce
1 (29 ounce) can diced tomatoes

1 (14½ ounce) can beef broth
2 tablespoons brown sugar
1 teaspoon salt
½ teaspoon pepper
1 tablespoon soy sauce
2 cups cooked rice

In a large pan, brown ground beef and onion. Drain. Add garlic and peppers and sauté for 3 minutes. Stir in the rest of ingredients, except rice. Reduce heat to low; cover and simmer for 30 to 45 minutes. Stir in rice and heat through.

CELEBRATIONS ON THE SIDE

O come all ye faithful,
Joyful and triumphant,
O come ye, O come ye to Bethlehem.

FREDERICK OAKELEY

WHITE AND WILD RICE MEDLEY

¼ cup butter or margarine
½ cup slivered almonds
¼ cup uncooked wild rice
1 (2½ ounce) jar sliced mushrooms, drained
2 tablespoons green onions, chopped
1 tablespoon instant chicken bouillon
2½ cups boiling water
¾ cup uncooked regular rice

Melt butter in skillet and add almonds, wild rice, mushrooms, and green onion. Cook and stir for 10 to 15 minutes until almonds are golden brown. Pour into ungreased 1½-quart casserole. Stir in instant bouillon and water. Cover and bake at 350 degrees for 30 minutes. Mix in regular rice. Cover and cook about 30 minutes longer until liquid is absorbed. Yield: 6 servings

CORN PUDDING

1 (16 ounce) can whole kernel corn, drained
1 (16 ounce) can cream-style corn
1 cup sour cream
½ cup butter, melted
2 eggs, beaten
1 (8.5 ounce) corn muffin mix
Pinch salt

Mix ingredients together. Pour into greased 2-quart baking dish. Bake at 350 degrees for 30 minutes or until golden brown.

CALICO BEANS

1 pound ground beef
1 medium onion, chopped
1 (16 ounce) can butter beans, drained
1 (16 ounce) can kidney beans, drained
1 (28 ounce) can pork and beans
1 cup brown sugar
1 cup ketchup
1 teaspoon mustard
1 teaspoon apple cider vinegar
4 slices of bacon, fried and crumbled

Brown ground beef and onion; drain. Mix all ingredients and bake 1 hour at 350 degrees.

HOLIDAY CRANBERRY CHUTNEY

1 (12 ounce) bag fresh or frozen cranberries
1 cup sugar
$^3/_4$ cup water
1 large apple, peeled, cored, and chopped
1 large pear, peeled, cored, and chopped
$^1/_2$ cup raisins
2 teaspoons cinnamon
1 teaspoon ginger
$^1/_4$ teaspoon cloves

In saucepan, combine all ingredients. Bring to boil, stirring constantly. Reduce heat; simmer for 15 to 20 minutes or until apples and pears are tender and mixture thickens. Cool completely. Store in refrigerator. Serve over cream cheese with crackers or as a condiment with pork, ham, or chicken.

SWEET POTATO SOUFFLÉ

3 cups mashed sweet potatoes
¾ cup brown sugar
1 (12 ounce) can evaporated milk
½ cup butter, melted
2 eggs
1½ teaspoons vanilla
½ teaspoon cinnamon
½ teaspoon salt

Topping:
1 cup chopped nuts (walnuts or pecans)
1 cup brown sugar
½ cup flour
½ cup butter, softened
½ cup flaked coconut, optional

Beat all ingredients, except topping, with electric mixer until well mixed. Place in greased 4-quart casserole dish. Mix topping and crumble over sweet potato mixture. Bake 350 degrees for 1 hour.

POTLUCK POTATOES

2 pounds frozen hash brown potatoes, thawed
½ cup butter, melted
1 (10¾ ounce) can cream of chicken soup
½ cup onion, chopped
1 teaspoon salt
½ teaspoon pepper

1 pint sour cream
2 cups processed cheese, cubed

Topping:
2 cups cornflakes, crushed
¼ cup melted butter

In large bowl, combine potatoes with butter. Heat soup, onion, salt, pepper, sour cream, and cheese until cheese is melted. Pour over potatoes and mix thoroughly. Pour into a greased 9x13-inch baking dish. Mix cornflakes and butter. Cover potato mixture with topping. Bake at 350 degrees for 1 hour.

OLD-FASHIONED POTATO CAKES

2 cups leftover mashed potatoes
1 egg, beaten
1 tablespoon flour
2 tablespoons heavy cream
1 tablespoon onion, minced

Mix everything together and drop by heaping tablespoonfuls in buttered skillet. Flatten with spatula. Turn when browned.

SPINACH MASHED POTATO BAKE

6 to 8 large potatoes, peeled and quartered
¾ cup sour cream
1 teaspoon sugar
½ cup butter
2 teaspoons salt
¼ teaspoon pepper
1 cup cheddar cheese, shredded
2 tablespoons chives, chopped
¼ teaspoon dill weed
1 box frozen chopped spinach, cooked and well drained

Cook and mash potatoes; add sour cream, sugar, butter, salt, and pepper. Beat until light and fluffy. Add chives, dill, and spinach. Place in greased 3-quart casserole dish; top with cheese. Bake at 400 degrees for 20 minutes. This is an excellent dish to prepare ahead of time and refrigerate. If refrigerated, bake at 400 degrees for 45 minutes or until heated through.

AMISH DRESSING

1 loaf bread
Butter
6 eggs, well beaten
2 cups milk
$\frac{1}{2}$ cup carrots, diced
$\frac{1}{2}$ cup celery, finely chopped
1 cup potatoes, cubed and boiled

1 cup chicken broth
Fresh parsley
$\frac{1}{4}$ cup onion, finely chopped
2 teaspoons chicken base or bouillon
2 teaspoons salt
$\frac{1}{4}$ teaspoon pepper
1 cup chicken, cooked and diced

Cube bread and toast in butter in a large skillet. Add remaining ingredients. Fry in butter until lightly browned. Transfer to large baking dish and bake at 325 degrees for 40 to 45 minutes.

HARVARD BEETS

3 (15 ounce) cans whole beets
2 tablespoons whole cloves
1 cup sugar
1 cup white vinegar
3 tablespoons butter
3 tablespoons ketchup
⅛ teaspoon salt
3 tablespoons cornstarch
1 teaspoon vanilla

Drain beets, reserving 1½ cups juice. Cut beets into wedges; set juice and beets aside. Place the cloves in spice bag and close. In large saucepan, combine sugar, vinegar, butter, ketchup, and salt. Add spice bag; bring to boil. Reduce heat; cover and simmer for 15 minutes. Discard spice bag. In small bowl, combine cornstarch and reserved beet juice until smooth. Stir in sugar mixture. Bring to boil; cook and stir 2 minutes or until thickened. Add beets and vanilla; heat through.

CREAMY SUCCOTASH

1 (10 ounce) package frozen corn
1 (10 ounce) package frozen cut green beans
1 (10 ounce) package frozen lima beans
1 large onion, chopped
1 or 2 stalks celery, chopped
1 (10¾ ounce) can cream of celery soup
1 teaspoon salt
Dash pepper
¼ teaspoon dried basil
¾ cup American cheese, cubed

Put all ingredients in greased 2-quart slow cooker. Mix well. Cover and cook on low for 6 to 8 hours or high 2½ to 3½ hours.

HONEY CASHEW GREEN BEANS

2 (16 ounce) bags frozen green beans
2 tablespoons cashews, coarsely chopped
4 tablespoons butter
1 tablespoon honey
1 drop almond flavoring, optional

Prepare beans according to directions. Meanwhile, in small skillet, sauté cashews in butter for about 5 minutes or until golden brown. Stir in honey and almond flavoring. Heat through. Pour over hot, drained green beans and toss to coat. Yield: 8 servings

TANGY RANCH GREEN BEANS

2 tablespoons butter
2 packages frozen French-cut green beans, partially thawed
1 can sliced mushrooms, drained
1 envelope ranch dressing mix
3 to 4 slices bacon, cooked and crumbled

In skillet, melt butter. Stir in green beans and cook until tender. Mix in mushrooms and ranch dressing mix. Heat through. Before serving, sprinkle crumbled bacon over beans.

CREAMY COLE SLAW

1 head cabbage, washed, drained, and shredded
1 medium carrot, shredded
¼ cup green pepper, finely chopped

Dressing:
1½ cups salad dressing
1 teaspoon salt
1 teaspoon mustard
⅓ cup sugar
2 teaspoons celery seed

Combine cabbage, carrot, and green pepper. Mix dressing ingredients and pour over cabbage mixture. Chill. Sprinkle with paprika before serving.

STRAWBERRY PRETZEL SALAD

2½ cups pretzels, crushed
¾ cup butter, melted
3 tablespoons brown sugar
1 (8 ounce) package cream cheese, softened
¾ cup sugar
1 (8 ounce) container whipped topping
1 (6 ounce) box strawberry gelatin mix
2 cups boiling water
2 (10 ounce) packages frozen strawberries

Combine pretzels, butter, and brown sugar. Press into bottom of 9x13-inch pan. Bake at 350 degrees for 10 minutes. Let cool. Cream together cream cheese and sugar; fold in whipped topping and spread over cooled crust. Make sure cream cheese mixture completely covers and seals crust. Dissolve gelatin in boiling water. Add strawberries.

Chill until thickened, but not set, stirring occasionally. When slightly thickened, pour over cream cheese mixture and chill until set.

Note: If using fresh strawberries, add additional 1½ cups cold water after gelatin is dissolved; continue as directed. Can also be prepared with raspberry gelatin and fresh or frozen raspberries.

BROCCOLI DELIGHT SALAD

5 cups fresh broccoli, chopped
1/2 cup raisins
1/4 cup red onion, chopped
3 tablespoons sugar
2 tablespoons vinegar
1 cup mayonnaise
10 bacon slices, fried and crumbled
1 cup sunflower seeds (optional)

In large bowl, mix broccoli, raisins, and onion. In small bowl, combine sugar, vinegar, and mayonnaise. Pour over broccoli; toss to coat. Refrigerate several hours. Sprinkle with bacon and sunflower seeds just before serving. Toss. Yield: 6 to 8 servings

SEVEN-LAYER SALAD

1 head lettuce, chopped
1 medium onion, chopped
1 (15 ounce) package frozen peas
1 pound bacon, fried and crumbled
¾ pound cheddar cheese, grated
8 hard-boiled eggs, sliced

Dressing:
¼ cup milk
1 cup mayonnaise
½ cup sugar
1½ teaspoons apple cider vinegar

Layer salad as listed in 9x13-inch glass baking dish. Mix dressing; pour over salad. Refrigerate several hours or overnight. Toss before serving.

EVERYONE'S FAVORITE APPLE SALAD

6 to 7 medium apples, peeled and diced
2 stalks celery, diced
½ cup walnuts or pecans, chopped
1 banana, sliced

Dressing:
2 tablespoons cornstarch
¾ cup sugar
1 egg, beaten
1 cup water or pineapple juice (or combination of both)
1 tablespoon apple cider vinegar
1 tablespoon butter
1 teaspoon vanilla

Mix diced apples, celery, nuts, and banana in bowl. In saucepan, whisk cornstarch and sugar together. Add egg and mix well. Whisk in water and vinegar. Bring to a boil, stirring constantly. When thickened and clear, remove from heat and add butter and vanilla. Cool. Pour cooled dressing over fruit and stir. Chill before serving.

CRANBERRY CHERRY SALAD

1 (14½ ounce) can pitted dark red
  cherries
1 (3 ounce) package cherry gelatin
1 (8 ounce) can jellied cranberry sauce
1 (3 ounce) package lemon gelatin
1 cup boiling water

3 ounces cream cheese, softened
⅓ cup mayonnaise
1 (8 ounce) can crushed pineapple,
  undrained
½ cup heavy whipping cream
1 cup miniature marshmallows

Drain cherries, reserving juice; set cherries aside. Add water to juice to measure 1 cup; transfer to saucepan. Bring to boil. Add cherry gelatin to boiling water; stir until dissolved. Whisk in cranberry sauce until smooth. Add cherries; pour into 7x11-inch dish. Refrigerate until firm. Dissolve lemon gelatin in boiling water. Beat softened cream cheese and mayonnaise. Gradually beat in lemon gelatin until smooth. Stir in pineapple. Refrigerate until almost set. Fold in whipped cream and marshmallows. Spoon over cherry layer. Refrigerate until firm.

DEVILED EGGS

6 hard, boiled eggs
3 tablespoons mayonnaise
2 teaspoons, sugar
⅛ teaspoon mustard
½ teaspoon apple cider vinegar
Pinch salt

Put eggs in pan of cold water. Water must cover eggs. Bring to a boil. Cook for 10 minutes. Drain off boiling water and add cold water to cool eggs. While slightly warm, peel eggs and cut in half lengthwise. Remove yolks and mash with fork. Add remaining ingredients and mix well. Spoon mixture back into egg white halves. Sprinkle with a little paprika for color. Yield: 12 servings

STAR ATTRACTIONS

But the angel said to them, "Do not be afraid. I bring you good news of great joy that will be for all the people. Today in the town of David a Savior has been born to you; he is Christ the Lord."

LUKE 2:10–11 NIV

CRANBERRY CHICKEN

6 boneless, skinless chicken breast halves
1 can whole-berry cranberry sauce
1 large Granny Smith apple, peeled and diced
½ cup raisins
1 teaspoon orange zest
¼ cup walnuts, chopped
1 teaspoon curry powder
1 teaspoon cinnamon

Place chicken in greased 9x13-inch baking dish. Bake at 350 degrees for 20 minutes. While chicken is cooking, combine remaining ingredients. Spoon cranberry mixture over chicken. Return to oven for 20 to 25 minutes or until chicken juices run clear.

BAKED CHICKEN BREASTS
IN CREAM SAUCE

4 boneless, skinless chicken breasts
4 slices Swiss cheese
1 (10¾ ounce) can condensed cream of chicken soup
¼ cup milk
2 cups chicken-flavored stuffing mix
¼ cup butter, melted

Place chicken in baking dish. Add cheese slice on top of each. Combine soup with milk; pour over chicken. Sprinkle with stuffing mix. Drizzle butter on top. Bake uncovered at 350 degrees for 1 hour.

PECAN CHICKEN CASSEROLE

2 cups cooked chicken, chopped
$\frac{1}{2}$ cup pecans, chopped
2 teaspoons minced onion
2 cups celery, chopped
1 cup mayonnaise
2 teaspoons lemon juice
1 cup potato chips, broken
$\frac{1}{2}$ cup cheddar cheese, shredded

Mix first 6 ingredients together. Place in greased 1½-quart casserole. Mix chips and cheese and sprinkle on top. Bake, uncovered, at 350 degrees for 30 minutes.

BUTTERMILK BAKED COD

1½ pounds cod fillets
½ cup butter, melted
1 teaspoon salt
1 teaspoon paprika
1 teaspoon garlic powder
1 teaspoon lemon juice
1 cup buttermilk
2 cups herb-flavored stuffing mix

Rinse and dry cod fillets; cut into serving pieces. Melt butter; add salt, paprika, garlic powder, and lemon juice. Set aside. Dip fish in buttermilk; roll in stuffing. Place in foil-lined 9x13-inch baking pan. Drizzle butter mixture over fish. Bake at 450 degrees for 10 to 15 minutes.

HONEY BAKED CHICKEN

3 to 4 pounds cut up chicken

Sauce:
⅔ cup butter, melted
⅔ cup honey
2 teaspoons salt
2 teaspoons curry powder
4 tablespoons mustard

Place chicken skin side up in baking dish. Combine sauce ingredients and pour over chicken. Bake at 250 degrees for 1½ hours or until chicken is tender. Baste every 15 minutes while baking. Sauce can be used on wings as well.

GLAZED HAM LOAF

¾ pound ground ham
¾ pound ground pork
⅔ cup bread crumbs
1 egg
1 cup milk

Sauce:
⅔ cup pineapple juice
½ cup brown sugar
2 tablespoons flour
1 teaspoon dry mustard
⅓ cup dark corn syrup
2 tablespoons vinegar

Mix ham, pork, bread crumbs, egg and milk together and put in loaf pan. Mix in saucepan; cook until thickened. Pour sauce over meat mixture. Bake 350 degrees for 1 hour. Let set for 5 minutes before slicing. Garnish with pineapple rings and maraschino cherries if desired.

SPAGHETTI PIE

½ pound spaghetti, cooked
¼ cup butter, melted
2 eggs, lightly beaten
½ cup Parmesan cheese
2 cups small curd cottage cheese
3 cups prepared spaghetti sauce, meat added
1 cup mozzarella cheese, grated

Mix together first four ingredients and press in greased pie pan. Layer cottage cheese over spaghetti and top with sauce. Bake 350 degrees for 30 minutes. Sprinkle with grated cheese and return to oven until cheese is melted. Let set 5 minutes and cut into pie slices.

DELICIOUS HERBED PORK ROAST

3 to 5 pound boneless pork loin roast
2 tablespoons olive oil
2 teaspoons dried marjoram
1 teaspoon salt
2 tablespoons sugar
$\frac{1}{2}$ teaspoon celery seed
2 teaspoons rubbed sage
$\frac{1}{8}$ teaspoon pepper
$\frac{1}{2}$ teaspoon ground mustard

Cover roast with olive oil, spreading evenly. Combine rest of ingredients; rub over meat. Cover and refrigerate for 4 hours or overnight. Place roast on rack in shallow roasting pan. Bake uncovered at 325 degrees for 2½ hours or until meat thermometer reads 160 degrees. Let rest 15 minutes before slicing.

REUBEN CASSEROLE

1½ cups Thousand Island dressing
1 cup sour cream
1 tablespoon onion, minced
1 to 1½ pounds deli-style corned beef, cut into bite-size pieces
1 pound Bavarian-style sauerkraut, drained
2½ cups Swiss cheese, shredded
8 to10 slices rye bread, cubed
¼ cup butter, melted

In a bowl mix Thousand Island dressing, sour cream, and onion. Layer corned beef and sauerkraut in bottom of greased 9x13-inch baking dish. Spread dressing mixture over corned beef mixture. Sprinkle with Swiss cheese, top with bread cubes, and drizzle with butter. Cover and bake 15 minutes at 350 degrees. Uncover and continue baking 10 minutes or until bubbly and lightly browned. Serve topped with additional Thousand Island dressing if desired.

MAPLE COUNTRY RIBS

3 pounds country-style pork ribs
1 cup pure maple syrup
½ cup applesauce
¼ cup ketchup
3 tablespoons lemon juice
¼ teaspoon salt
¼ teaspoon pepper
¼ teaspoon paprika
¼ teaspoon garlic powder
¼ teaspoon cinnamon

Place ribs in large kettle or Dutch oven. Cover with water and bring to a boil. Reduce heat and simmer for 10 minutes. Drain. Place ribs in greased 9x13-inch baking dish. Combine remaining ingredients; pour half over ribs. Bake uncovered at 325 degrees for 1½ hours or until tender, basting often with remaining sauce. Yield: 4 servings

TASTES-LIKE-HOME MEATLOAF

1½ cups quick-cooking oats
1½ cups milk
3 eggs, beaten
3 pounds lean ground beef
1 tablespoon salt
½ cup onion, chopped
½ teaspoon black pepper

Sauce:
¾ cup ketchup
½ cup brown sugar
1 teaspoon mustard

Combine oats, milk, and beaten eggs. Let soak for 5 minutes. Add remaining ingredients and mix thoroughly. Pack firmly into loaf pan or form loaf in baking dish. Pour sauce over meatloaf and bake 1 hour and 15 minutes at 350 degrees. Let set 10 minutes before slicing.

ORANGE-GLAZED CORNISH HENS

4 (22 ounce) Cornish game hens
$1/4$ cup butter, melted
1 teaspoon salt
$1/2$ teaspoon pepper
$3/4$ cup orange juice
$1/2$ cup brown sugar
$1/2$ cup sherry or chicken broth
2 tablespoons lemon juice
1 teaspoon ground mustard
$1/4$ teaspoon ground allspice

Tie legs of each hen together with cooking twine. Place on a greased rack in roasting pan. Brush with butter; sprinkle with salt and pepper. Bake, uncovered, at 350 degrees for 1 hour. In a saucepan, combine the remaining ingredients; bring to boil. Reduce heat; simmer, uncovered, for 15 minutes. Spoon over hens. Bake 15 minutes or until meat thermometer reads 180 degrees.

PARTY CHICKEN

½ cup Dijon mustard
½ cup honey
4½ teaspoons vegetable oil, divided
½ teaspoon lemon juice
4 boneless, skinless chicken breast halves
¼ teaspoon salt
⅛ teaspoon pepper
Dash paprika
2 cups fresh mushrooms
2 tablespoons butter
1 cup Monterey Jack cheese, shredded
1 cup cheddar cheese, shredded
8 bacon strips, partially cooked
2 teaspoons fresh parsley, minced

Combine mustard, honey, 1½ teaspoons oil, and lemon juice. Pour ½ cup of mixture in large resealable bag; add chicken. Seal bag and turn to coat; refrigerate for 2 hours. Refrigerate remaining marinade. After marinade time is up, drain and discard marinade from chicken. Heat remaining oil in large skillet; brown chicken on all sides. Sprinkle with salt, pepper, and paprika. Transfer to greased 7x11-inch baking dish. In same skillet, sauté mushrooms in butter until tender. Spoon reserved marinade over chicken. Top with cheeses and mushrooms. Place bacon strips in crisscross pattern over chicken. Bake uncovered at 375 degrees for 20 to 25 minutes. Sprinkle with parsley.

SALMON WITH CREAMY DILL SAUCE

1 salmon fillet (about 2 pounds)
1 teaspoon lemon-pepper seasoning
1 teaspoon onion salt
1 small onion, sliced and separated
    into rings
6 lemon slices
¼ cup butter

Dill Sauce:
⅓ cup sour cream
⅓ cup mayonnaise
1 tablespoon onion, finely chopped
1 teaspoon lemon juice
1 teaspoon horseradish
¾ teaspoon dill weed
¼ teaspoon garlic salt

Line a 10x15-inch baking pan with heavy-duty foil; grease lightly. Place salmon skin side down on foil. Sprinkle with lemon-pepper and onion salt. Top with onion and lemon. Dot with butter. Fold foil around salmon; seal tightly. Bake at 350 degrees for 20 minutes. Open foil. Broil 4 to 6 inches from heat 8 to 12 minutes or until fish flakes easily with a fork. Combine sauce ingredients until smooth. Serve with salmon.

TRADITIONAL HOLIDAY
HAM WITH PINEAPPLE

1 (12 to14 pound) whole bone-in fully cooked ham, spiral cut or thinly sliced
2 (6 ounce) cans pineapple juice
1 (20 ounce) can crushed pineapple, undrained
2 cups brown sugar
20 to 30 whole cloves
¼ cup golden raisins

Place ham in roasting pan. Slowly pour pineapple juice over ham so it runs between slices. Spoon pineapple over ham. Sprinkle with brown sugar and cloves. Add raisins to pan juices. Cover and bake at 325 degrees for 1½ to 2 hours or until a meat thermometer reads 140 degrees, basting every 20 minutes. Yield: 24 to 28 servings

STUFFED CROWN ROAST OF PORK

1 (5 to 6 pound) pork loin crown roast
½ teaspoon seasoned salt

Mushroom Stuffing:
1 cup fresh mushrooms, sliced
½ cup celery, diced
¼ cup butter
3 cups day-old bread cubes
¼ teaspoon salt
¼ teaspoon pepper
½ cup chicken broth
⅓ cup apricot preserves
1 cup whole fresh cranberries, optional

Place roast, rib ends up, in shallow roasting pan; sprinkle with seasoned salt. Cover rib ends with foil. Bake, uncovered, at 325 degrees for 1½ hours. Meanwhile, sauté mushrooms and celery in butter until tender. Stir in bread cubes, salt, pepper, and chicken broth. Spoon into center of roast. Brush sides of roast with preserves. Bake 1 hour longer or until meat thermometer inserted into meat between ribs reads 160 degrees; remove foil. Transfer to serving platter. If desired, string cranberries on a 20-inch piece of string. Loop cranberry string in and out of the rib ends.

MISS MANDY'S STUFFED SHELLS

1 (30 ounce) container ricotta cheese or
  2 cups mozzarella cheese
1 cup Parmesan cheese
2 eggs
1 to 3 cloves garlic, minced
2 to 3 tablespoons parsley
1 box large pasta shells, cooked and drained
1 (10 ounce) jar of your favorite spaghetti sauce

Mix ricotta or mozzarella cheese, Parmesan cheese, eggs, garlic, and parsley with electric mixer until smooth. Chill. Stuff mixture into cooked shells. Spread a thin layer of spaghetti sauce on bottom of greased 9x13-inch baking dish. Place shells on sauce. Spoon additional sauce over shells. Bake 350 degrees for 30 to 40 minutes. Sprinkle with additional Parmesan cheese and parsley if desired.

HERB RIB ROAST WITH PEPPERY HORSERADISH SAUCE

1 (4 pound) beef rib roast
1 clove garlic, peeled and cut in half
¼ cup Dijon mustard
¾ cup fresh parsley, chopped

1½ teaspoons dried thyme
1½ teaspoons dried rosemary
2 cloves garlic, finely chopped
1 tablespoon olive or vegetable oil

Place beef roast, fat side up, on rack in shallow roasting pan. Rub roast with garlic halves. Spread mustard over top and sides of roast. Mix together remaining ingredients except oil; stir in oil. Spread herb mixture over top and sides of roast. Insert meat thermometer in thickest part of roast, not touching bone. Roast uncovered about 1½ to 2 hours for medium doneness (160 degrees). Cover roast loosely with foil tent and let stand about 15 minutes before carving. Serve with peppery horseradish sauce (page 104).

PEPPERY HORSERADISH SAUCE

1 cup sour cream
1 tablespoon plus 1 teaspoon horseradish
1 tablespoon plus 1 teaspoon Dijon mustard

Mix all ingredients. Cover and refrigerate at least 1 hour to blend flavors.

FESTIVE BARS & COOKIES

When we were children, we were grateful to those who filled our stockings at Christmas time. Why are we not grateful to God for filling our stockings with legs?

G. K. CHESTERTON

PUMPKIN PECAN PIE SQUARES

Crust:
2½ cups flour
1 cup cold butter
½ cup brown sugar
½ teaspoon salt

Filling:
4 eggs
1½ cups light corn syrup
1½ cups sugar
3 tablespoons butter, melted
1½ teaspoons vanilla
2½ cups pecans, chopped

At medium speed, mix all ingredients for crust until mixture resembles fine crumbs. Press in greased 9x13-inch pan. Bake at 350 degrees for 20 minutes, or until golden brown. While crust is baking, prepare filling. Beat eggs, corn syrup, sugar, butter, and vanilla until well blended. Stir in pecans. Pour filling over hot crust. Bake 25 minutes or until filling is slightly firm in center. Cool and cut.

PECAN PIE SQUARES

Crust:
1 cup flour
½ cup quick oats
½ cup brown sugar
½ cup butter, softened

Filling:
¾ cup sugar

1 (15 ounce) can pumpkin
1 (12 ounce) can evaporated milk
2 eggs
2¼ teaspoons pumpkin pie spice

Topping:
½ cup pecans, chopped
¼ cup brown sugar

Combine crust ingredients with mixer until crumbly. Press in bottom of greased 9x13-inch baking pan.

Beat sugar, pumpkin, evaporated milk, eggs, and pumpkin pie spice at medium speed for 1 to 2 minutes; pour over crust. Bake 20 minutes at 350 degrees.

Topping: Combine pecans and brown sugar; sprinkle over filling. Continue baking 15 minutes or until knife inserted in center comes out clean. Cool and cut into bars. Top with whipped cream.

CREAM CHEESE BARS

½ cup butter
1 (18.25 ounce) box yellow cake mix
3½ cups powdered sugar
2 eggs
1 (8 ounce) package cream cheese, softened

Mix butter and cake mix until crumbly. Pat in a greased 9x13-inch pan. Cream powdered sugar, eggs, and cream cheese. Spread over cake mix crust. Bake at 350 degress for 35 minutes.

BERRY SHORTBREAD DREAMS

1 cup butter, softened
⅔ cup sugar
1 ounce cream cheese, softened
½ teaspoon almond extract
2 cups flour
½ cup raspberry or strawberry jam

Glaze:
1 cup powdered sugar
1 teaspoon vanilla or almond flavoring
2 to 3 teaspoons hot water

Cream butter, sugar, and cream cheese. Add almond extract and flour. Refrigerate 1 hour. Shape into 1-inch balls. Make an indentation in the middle with your thumb. Fill with jam. Bake at 350 degrees 7 to 9 minutes or until golden brown. Cool, then drizzle with glaze. Yield: about 3 dozen cookies

HARVEST PUMPKIN BARS

4 eggs, slightly beaten
1 cup vegetable oil
1 (15 ounce) can pumpkin
2 cups sugar
2 teaspoons cinnamon
1 teaspoon baking soda
1 teaspoon baking powder
2 cups flour
1 teaspoon salt
1 cup nuts, chopped

Mix together all ingredients and pour into greased jelly roll pan. Bake at 350 degrees
20 to 25 minutes or until inserted toothpick comes out clean. Frost with Cream
Cheese Icing (page 111).

CREAM CHEESE ICING

3 ounces cream cheese, softened
6 tablespoons butter, melted
1 tablespoon milk
1 teaspoon vanilla
3½ cups powdered sugar

Beat cream cheese until smooth; add rest of ingredients and beat until well mixed. Spread on bars while slightly warm. Sprinkle with more chopped nuts if desired. Cut into bars.

MONSTER COOKIES

1 cup butter
2 cups brown sugar
2 cups sugar
6 eggs
2 teaspoons vanilla
1 tablespoon light corn syrup

4 teaspoons baking soda
3 cups peanut butter
9 cups quick oats
$\frac{1}{2}$ pound semisweet chocolate chips
$\frac{1}{2}$ pound chocolate-coated candy

Cream butter and sugars; add eggs, vanilla, corn syrup, soda, and peanut butter. Add oats; mix well. Add chocolate chips and candies. Drop by cookie scoop onto cookie sheet. Bake at 350 degrees 8 to 10 minutes. Do not overbake.

CHEWY PEANUT BARS

1 (16.5 ounce) refrigerated tube sugar
   cookie dough
3 cups miniature marshmallows
$2/3$ cup light corn syrup
$1/4$ cup butter

$1\frac{1}{2}$ teaspoons vanilla
1 (10 ounce) bag peanut butter chips
2 cups crisp rice cereal
2 cups salted peanuts

With floured fingers, press cookie dough in bottom of ungreased 9x13-inch baking dish. Bake at 350 degrees for 12 to 15 minutes or until golden brown. Sprinkle marshmallows evenly over hot crust. Return to oven; bake 1 minute longer or until marshmallows just begin to puff up. Remove from oven and cool while making topping. In large saucepan, heat corn syrup, butter, vanilla, and peanut butter chips. Stir constantly until melted and smooth. Remove from heat; stir in cereal and peanuts. Immediately spoon warm topping over marshmallows; spread to cover. Refrigerate until firm. Cut into bars.

COCONUT DATE BALLS

1 cup sugar

½ cup butter

1 egg, beaten

1 cup dates, finely chopped

1 teaspoon vanilla

3 cups crisp rice cereal

½ cup walnuts, chopped

Flaked coconut

Powdered sugar

Combine first 5 ingredients in saucepan; cook until thickened, stirring constantly. Remove from heat. Add in rice cereal and walnuts. Cool and roll into 1½-inch balls. Roll in coconut flakes and powdered sugar.

CHOCOLATE RIVAL BARS

1 cup butter, softened
2 cups brown sugar
2 eggs
2 teaspoons vanilla
2½ cups flour
1 teaspoon baking soda
½ teaspoon salt
3 cups quick oats

Filling:
1 (12 ounce) package milk chocolate
  chips
1 (14 ounce) can sweetened condensed
  milk
2 teaspoons butter
2 teaspoons vanilla
¼ teaspoon salt

Cream butter and sugar until light and fluffy. Add eggs and vanilla. Beat well. Stir in dry ingredients. Pat ⅔ of dough into greased 10x15-inch jelly roll pan. Combine filling ingredients in saucepan and stir over low heat until smooth. Spread filling over top. Drop remaining dough over chocolate layer. Bake at 350 degrees for 20 to 25 minutes or until light golden brown. Cut into bars when cool.

SOUR CREAM COOKIES

½ cup shortening
1½ cups sugar
2 eggs
1 teaspoon vanilla
1 cup sour cream
2¾ cups flour
½ teaspoon baking soda
½ teaspoon baking powder
½ teaspoon salt

Frosting:
½ cup butter, softened
2 teaspoons vanilla
2½ cups powdered sugar
¼ cup milk

Cream shortening and sugar; add eggs, vanilla, and sour cream. In separate bowl, whisk dry ingredients. Gradually add flour mixture to butter mixture. Mix until blended. Drop by tablespoonfuls onto cookie sheet. Bake at 350 degrees for 8 to 10 minutes. Cool. Ice with frosting.

Frosting: Beat together all ingredients with mixer until smooth.

CORNFLAKE CRUNCHIES

1 cup sugar
1 cup light corn syrup
1 cup peanut butter
1 cup pretzel sticks, broken
1 cup peanuts
5 cups cornflakes

Mix sugar and corn syrup in saucepan. Bring to a boil. Remove from heat; add peanut butter and stir until melted. Stir in pretzels, nuts, and cornflakes. Mix well. Drop by teaspoonfuls onto waxed paper. Cool.

ASHLEY'S PEANUT BUTTER BLOSSOMS

1 cup butter, softened
1 cup sugar
1 cup brown sugar
1 cup peanut butter
2 eggs
¼ cup milk

2 teaspoons vanilla
3½ cups flour
2 teaspoons baking soda
1 teaspoon salt
Chocolate kisses

Cream butter, sugars, and peanut butter. Add eggs, milk, and vanilla. Whisk flour, soda, and salt together; mix into peanut butter mixture. Chill thoroughly. Shape into walnut-size balls and roll in additional sugar. Bake at 350 degrees for 8 to 10 minutes. Press chocolate kiss in center of each cookie while still warm.

GRANDMA'S MOLASSES COOKIES

¾ cup butter
1 cup sugar
1 egg
1 tablespoon orange juice
¼ cup molasses
¼ teaspoon salt

½ teaspoon ground cloves
¾ teaspoon cinnamon
1 teaspoon ginger
1 teaspoon baking soda
2¼ cups flour
2 tablespoons sugar

Cream butter and 1 cup sugar until light and fluffy. Beat in egg, orange juice, and molasses. Whisk dry ingredients together and stir into molasses mixture. Chill dough. Shape dough into 1-inch balls and roll them in remaining 2 tablespoons sugar. Place 2 inches apart on cookie sheet and bake 8 to 10 minutes at 350 degrees.

JOHN'S FAVORITE FROSTED ORANGE COOKIES

1 cup butter, softened
2 cups sugar
2 eggs
1 cup sour cream
¾ cup orange juice concentrate, thawed

2 tablespoons fresh grated orange zest
1 teaspoon salt
1 teaspoon baking soda
2 teaspoons baking powder
5½ cups flour

Cream butter and sugar; add eggs, sour cream, orange juice, and zest. Beat well. Whisk together rest of ingredients. Add to wet and blend. Drop onto cookie sheets by teaspoonfuls or use cookie scoop. Bake at 350 degrees for 8 to 10 minutes. Frost cookies when cooled.

Frosting:
4 tablespoons butter, softened
2 tablespoons orange juice concentrate, thawed
½ teaspoon fresh orange zest
1½ cups powdered sugar

Beat all ingredients until smooth and fluffy. You may need to adjust the amount of powdered sugar to make frosting the right consistency.

RUSSIAN TEA CAKES

1 cup butter
½ cup powdered sugar
2¼ cups flour
½ cup pecans, finely chopped
¼ teaspoon salt
1 teaspoon vanilla
Additional powdered sugar

Combine all ingredients; mix well. Refrigerate dough until chilled. Roll dough into 1-inch balls and bake 10 to 15 minutes at 350 degrees. Remove from oven and roll in powdered sugar. Let cool slightly and roll in powdered sugar a second time.

SWEET ENDINGS

Our hearts grow tender with childhood memories and love of kindred, and we are better throughout the year for having, in spirit, become a child again at Christmastime.

LAURA INGALLS WILDER

LEMON DELIGHT

Crust:
½ cup butter
1 cup flour
½ cup walnuts or pecans, chopped

Mix and press into 9x13-inch pan. Bake at 375 degrees for 12 to 15 minutes. Cool.

Filling:
1 (8 ounce) package cream cheese, softened
1 cup powdered sugar
1 cup whipped topping

Beat cream cheese until smooth; add sugar and whipped topping. Beat until mixed. Spread on top of crust.

Pudding:
2 (3 ounce) packages lemon instant pudding
3 cups milk

Combine pudding mix and milk. Beat until mixture thickens. Pour over cream cheese mixture. Top with additional 2 cups whipped topping. Chill.

APPLE CRISP

1 cup flour
¾ cup oatmeal
1 cup brown sugar
1 teaspoon cinnamon
½ cup butter, melted
4 cups apples, diced
1 cup sugar
2 tablespoons cornstarch
1 cup water
1 teaspoon vanilla

Mix flour, oatmeal, brown sugar, and cinnamon. Work in butter with a fork until crumbly. Press half of crumbs in a greased 9x9-inch baking dish. Cover with diced apples. Cook the sugar, cornstarch, and water until clear and thick. Remove from heat and add vanilla. Pour over apples. Top with remaining crumbs. Bake at 350 degrees for 1 hour.

HEAVENLY HOT FUDGE SAUCE

¹/₂ cup butter
4 ounces unsweetened chocolate
3 cups sugar
¹/₂ teaspoon salt
1 (12 ounce) can evaporated milk

Melt butter and chocolate together over low heat. Add sugar and salt. Mix well. Slowly stir in evaporated milk. Continue stirring and bring to boil. Delicious served over ice cream.

EGGNOG CHEESECAKE

Crust:
2 cups vanilla wafer crumbs
6 tablespoons butter, melted
½ teaspoon nutmeg

Filling:
4 (8 ounce) packages cream cheese, softened
1 cup sugar
3 tablespoons flour
3 tablespoons rum flavoring
1 teaspoon vanilla
2 eggs
1 cup whipping cream
4 egg yolks

To make crust, mix crumbs, butter, and nutmeg. Press into bottom and up sides of a 9-inch springform pan. Bake at 325 degrees for 10 minutes. For filling, beat cream cheese until smooth. Add sugar, flour, rum flavoring, and vanilla with electric mixer at medium speed until well blended. Add eggs, one at a time, mixing on low speed after each addition, just until blended. Blend in cream and egg yolks; pour over crust. Bake 1 hour to 1 hour and 15 minutes or until center is almost set. Run knife around rim of pan to loosen cake; cool before removing rim of pan. Refrigerate 4 hours or overnight. Garnish with whipped topping and sprinkle with nutmeg. Yield: 12 servings

MINI CHEESECAKES

2 (8 ounce) packages cream cheese, softened
¾ cup sugar
2 eggs
1 teaspoon vanilla
24 vanilla wafer cookies
Fruit pie filling

Beat cream cheese until smooth. Add sugar, eggs, and vanilla. Beat until well mixed. Place muffin liners in muffin tins. Lay a vanilla wafer cookie flat side down in each paper liner. Pour cream cheese mixture on top until ¾ full. Bake at 375 degrees for 12 minutes. Let cool. Top with a spoonful of favorite fruit pie filling. Refrigerate.

DELICATE LEMON SQUARES

Crust:
1 cup flour
¼ cup powdered sugar
½ cup butter

Filling:
2 eggs
¾ cup sugar
3 tablespoons fresh lemon juice
2 tablespoons flour
½ teaspoon baking powder
Powdered sugar

Crust: Mix flour and powdered sugar and cut in butter until mixture clings together. Press into an ungreased 8x8-inch baking pan; bake at 350 degrees for 10 to12 minutes.

Filling: In another mixing bowl beat eggs; add sugar and lemon juice and beat until thick and smooth—about 8 to 10 minutes. Stir together flour and baking powder and add to egg mixture, blending until all ingredients are moistened. Pour egg mixture gently over baked crust. Bake at 350 degrees for 20 to 25 minutes. Cool slightly and sift powdered sugar over top. When cool, cut cookies into1½-inch squares.

TIRAMISU TOFFEE DESSERT

1 (10.75 ounce) pound cake, cut into 9 slices
¾ cup strong coffee
1 (8 ounce) package cream cheese, softened
1 cup sugar
½ cup chocolate-flavored syrup
2 cups heavy whipping cream
2 (1.4 ounce) chocolate-covered toffee candy bars, chopped

Arrange cake slices on bottom of 7x11-inch baking dish cutting slices as necessary to cover bottom of dish. Drizzle coffee over cake. Beat cream cheese until smtooth; add sugar and chocolate syrup. Mix well. Add whipping cream and beat until light and fluffy. Spread over cake. Sprinkle with candy. Cover and refrigerate at least 1 hour to set dessert and blend flavors.

PECAN TASSIES

Crust:
6 ounces cream cheese, softened
1 cup butter, softened
2¼ cups flour
¼ teaspoon salt

Filling:
3 eggs, slightly beaten
1½ cups brown sugar
3 tablespoons butter, melted
1 teaspoon vanilla
½ cup pecans or walnuts, chopped

In mixing bowl, beat cream cheese and butter; blend in flour and salt. Chill 1 hour. Shape into 1-inch balls; press in bottom and up the sides of greased mini-muffin pan. Beat eggs in small mixing bowl. Add brown sugar, butter, and vanilla; mix well. Stir in pecans. Fill crusts with mixture. Bake at 325 degrees for 25 to 30 minutes.

RACHELLE'S CHOCOLATE CAKE TRUFFLES

1 box chocolate cake mix
$\frac{1}{2}$ cup butter, melted
$\frac{1}{2}$ cup powdered sugar
$\frac{1}{2}$ cup cocoa
$\frac{1}{2}$ cup walnuts or hazelnuts, finely chopped
2 teaspoons bourbon, optional
1 pound semisweet or milk chocolate, melted

Bake cake according to directions on box. Cool. Crumble baked cake into fine crumbs in mixing bowl. Add remaining ingredients; mix well. Roll into 1-inch balls; dip into melted chocolate. Cool on waxed paper.

HOMEMADE APPLE DUMPLINGS

Sauce:
2 cups sugar
2 cups water
½ teaspoon cinnamon
¼ cup butter

Crust:
2 cups flour
2½ teaspoons baking
   powder
½ teaspoon salt
⅔ cup shortening
½ cup milk

Filling (per apple):
dab of butter
1 teaspoon brown sugar
Dash cinnamon
3 apples, peeled, halved,
   and cored

Mix sauce ingredients in saucepan; simmer for 5 minutes and set aside. Mix flour, baking powder, and salt, then cut in the shortening until it forms small beads. Add milk. Roll and cut into 5-inch squares. Place an apple on each square and fill center of the apple with filling ingredients. Wrap dough over apple; pinch to seal. Arrange dumplings in greased 9x13-inch baking dish. Pour sauce over each dumpling. Bake at 375 degrees for 35 to 40 minutes. Baste several times while baking. Yield: 6 servings

DATE PUDDING WITH CARAMEL SAUCE

Cake:
1 cup dates, chopped
1 cup boiling water
1 tablespoon butter
1 teaspoon baking soda
¼ teaspoon salt
1 cup sugar
1½ cups flour
½ cup walnuts, chopped
1 egg, beaten

Caramel Sauce:
2 tablespoons butter
1 cup brown sugar
2 cups water
2 tablespoons cornstarch
¼ teaspoon salt
Water
1 tablespoon vanilla

Pour 1 cup boiling water over dates, butter, and soda; let set until cooled. Add remaining ingredients. Pour into greased 9x9-inch cake pan. Bake at 350 degrees 20 to 25 minutes. Cool; cut into cubes.

Carmel Sauce: Brown butter in saucepan. Add brown sugar and 2 cups water; heat to boiling. In small bowl, stir together cornstarch, salt, and enough water to make smooth paste. Add to sugar mixture and cook until clear, stirring constantly. Remove from heat; add vanilla. Cool. Cut cooled cake into squares and layer with whipped cream and caramel sauce. Banana slices are optional. Looks nice in a trifle bowl.

MERRY BERRY COBBLER

3 cups fresh or frozen fruit (raspberries, blueberries, cherries, etc.)
1¾ cups sugar, divided
1 teaspoon baking powder
¼ teaspoon salt
1 cup flour

3 tablespoons butter, softened
½ cup milk
1 tablespoon cornstarch
1 cup boiling water

Place fruit in bottom of greased 9x9-inch baking dish. Whisk together ¾ cup sugar, baking powder, salt, and flour. With fork, blend in butter until coarse crumbs form. Add milk; mix gently. Spoon dough over fruit. Mix remaining 1 cup sugar and cornstarch. Sprinkle over dough. Pour boiling water slowly over dough. Sprinkle with nutmeg. Bake at 350 degrees for 1 hour.

TOFFEE BAR CAKE

1 box German chocolate cake mix
1 (14 ounce) can sweetened condensed milk
1 jar caramel ice cream topping
1 (8 ounce) container whipped topping, thawed
3 to 6 chocolate toffee candy bars, crushed

Bake cake according to package directions. While cake is still hot, poke holes in cake about 1 inch apart using handle of wooden spoon. Blend together sweetened condensed milk and ice cream topping, then pour mixture over cake, making sure cake is completely covered. Refrigerate overnight. Before serving, garnish with whipped topping and sprinkle with toffee candy bar crumbs.

Note: Candy bars can be easily crushed by freezing first, then breaking with a hammer.

APPLE CINNAMON CAKE
WITH CREAM SAUCE

³/₄ cup butter
1¹/₂ cups sugar
2 eggs
3 medium apples, finely diced
¹/₂ teaspoon salt
1¹/₂ cups flour

1¹/₂ teaspoons cinnamon
1 teaspoon baking soda
1 teaspoon baking powder
¹/₂ cup walnuts, chopped

Cream butter and sugar. Add eggs and mix well. Add remaining ingredients and beat until well mixed. Pour into greased 9x13-inch baking dish. Bake at 325 degrees for 40 to 45 minutes.

Cream Sauce:
1 cup butter
2 cups sugar
1 cup light cream or half & half
2 teaspoons vanilla

Combine ingredients in medium saucepan and heat until thickened. Cut cake while still warm. Pour cream sauce over piece of cake as served. Delicious served warm with vanilla ice cream.

YUMMY GINGERBREAD
WITH LEMON SAUCE

½ cup butter, softened
½ cup sugar
1 cup molasses
1 egg
1½ teaspoons baking soda
1 teaspoon ginger

1 teaspoon cinnamon
½ teaspoon ground cloves
½ teaspoon salt
2½ cups flour
1 cup hot coffee

Cream butter; add sugar and beat well. Add molasses and egg. Mix well. Whisk together dry ingredients and add to creamed mixture. Blend in hot coffee and pour into greased 9x13-inch pan. Bake at 350 degrees for 30 to 40 minutes. Serve warm with lemon sauce and whipped cream.

LEMON SAUCE

¾ cup sugar
1 egg, beaten
4 tablespoons butter
¼ cup water
2 tablespoons fresh lemon juice
Zest of one lemon

In medium saucepan, combine sugar and egg. Add butter and water; cook over medium heat until mixture begins to boil. Boil for 1 minute or until slightly thickened. Stir in lemon juice and zest.

OATMEAL CAKE

1½ cups boiling water
1 cup quick oats
½ cup butter
1 cup brown sugar
1 cup sugar
2 eggs, well beaten

1 teaspoon vanilla
1¾ cups flour
1 teaspoon baking powder
1 teaspoon baking soda
½ teaspoon salt
1 teaspoon cinnamon

Combine boiling water and quick oats and let cool while mixing the rest of the cake. Mix remaining ingredients together. Add oatmeal mixture and beat well. Bake at 350 degrees for 25 to 30 minutes.

Topping:
1 tablespoon light corn syrup
1 cup brown sugar
¼ cup butter
½ cup cream or half & half
1 cup flaked coconut
½ cup pecans, chopped

Bring corn syrup, brown sugar, butter, and cream to boil. Add coconut and nuts. Spread on hot cake and return to oven under broiler until icing is bubbly and slightly browned.

TURTLE CAKE

¾1 Box German choccolate cake mix
1(14 ounce) bag caramels, unwrapped
¾ cup butter
½ cup evaporated milk
1 cup semisweet chocolate chips
1 cup pecans, chopped

Mix cake accoding to diections Pour half of cake batter into greased 9x13-inch cake pan. Bake at 350 degress for 12 to 15 minutes. In saucepan over low heat, melt caramels, butter, and milk, Pour caramel mixture over half-baked cake. Sprinkle with choclate chips and pecans. Pour second half of batter over the top and bake additional 20 minutes. when cool, sprinkle with powdered sugar.

JESSICA'S MANDARIN ORANGE CAKE

1 box yellow cake mix
¼ cup oil

1 (11 ounce) can mandarin oranges,
with juice
4 eggs

Beat cake mix, oil, oranges, and eggs with electric mixer 2 minutes. Divide batter into three 9-inch round greased cake pans. Bake at 350 degrees for 15 to 20 minutes. Cool completely and frost between layers, sides, and top.

Frosting:
1 (3.5 ounce) package vanilla instant pudding mix
1 (20 ounce) can crushed pineapple, with juice
1 (8 ounce) container whipped topping

Beat pudding mix and pineapple. Fold in whipped topping. Ice cooled cake and refrigerate before serving.

PEANUT BUTTER CREAM PIE

3 cups milk
⅔ cup sugar
6 tablespoons flour
½ teaspoon salt
3 egg yolks, slightly beaten

1½ teaspoons vanilla
1 tablespoon butter

Crumbs:
⅔ cup peanut butter
⅓ cup powdered sugar

Heat milk just to boiling; remove from heat. Mix together the sugar, flour, and salt. Add 1 cup of hot milk to sugar mixture; stir until smooth. Add slightly beaten egg yolks to mixture. Pour slowly into remainder of hot milk. Stir over medium heat until thick. Boil 2 to 3 minutes, stirring constantly. Remove from heat; add butter and vanilla. Cool. Mix crumb ingredients together with fork. Layer crumbs in bottom of baked pie shell, reserving some to garnish top of pie. Spread cooled pudding over crumbs. Top with whipped topping. Sprinkle reserved crumbs on top. Refrigerate until firm.

CHOCOLATE SILK PIE

¾ cup butter
1 cup sugar
2 ounces unsweetened chocolate,
  melted
1 teaspoon vanilla
3 eggs

Topping:
1 cup heavy cream
2 tablespoons powdered sugar
½ teaspoon vanilla
Chocolate curls

Cream butter and sugar until light and fluffy. Add chocolate and vanilla; beat on high until sugar is dissolved. Add eggs one at a time, beating on high for 2 minutes after each addition. Spoon into baked 9-inch pie crust. In a separate bowl, beat cream and powdered sugar until stiff peaks form. Fold in vanilla. Cover top of pie with whipped cream and garnish with chocolate curls. Chill.

BREAD PUDDING WITH WHITE CHOCOLATE SAUCE

6 slices day-old bread
2 tablespoons butter, melted
4 eggs, beaten
2 cups milk

¾ cup sugar
1 teaspoon cinnamon
1 teaspoon vanilla

Break bread into small pieces and place in 8x8-inch baking dish. Drizzle with butter. In medium mixing bowl, combine eggs, milk, sugar, cinnamon, and vanilla. Beat until well mixed. Pour over bread and lightly push down with a fork until bread is covered and soaking up egg mixture. Bake at 350 degrees for 45 minutes or until top springs back when lightly touched. Serve warm with white chocolate sauce.

Note: Flavored creamer can be substituted for half of milk. If substituting milk with creamer, add less sugar.

White Chocolate Sauce:
¾ cup heavy whipping cream
6 ounces white chocolate chips

Microwave cream on high for 1 minute or until it starts to simmer. Remove and add chocolate; stir until smooth.

RAISIN CREAM PIE

2 cups milk
3 tablespoons flour
1 cup sugar
1 teaspoon salt
4 egg yolks, well beaten
2 tablespoons butter
1¼ cup raisins
2 teaspoons vanilla
Whipped cream or graham cracker crumbs

Heat milk in saucepan. Mix flour, sugar, salt, and egg yolks; add a little hot milk to temper it. Stir into remaining hot milk. Boil until thickened, stirring constantly. Add butter and raisins and cook stirring constantly. When thickened, remove from heat and add vanilla. Cool. Spread in bottom of baked pie shell. Top with whipped cream or graham cracker crumbs.

INDEX